THE BEST 50

BUTTERMILK

RECIPES

Christie Katona
Thomas Katona

BRISTOL PUBLISHING ENTERPRISES
San Leandro, California

Printed in the United States of America.

ISBN 1-55867-115-3

Cover design: Frank Paredes
Cover photography: John Benson
Food stylist: Suzanne Carreiro

BUTTERMILK FACTS

Buttermilk has a down-home country feel and conjures up a picture of a white-haired grandma busily baking in her kitchen, preparing a host of wonderfully smelling biscuits and desserts for her visiting relatives. When we think of buttermilk, we think of biscuits, pancakes and, yes, butter. Like most youths raised in the city, we used to believe buttermilk contained large quantities of butter. After all, it was named *butter*milk, wasn't it? However, nothing could be further from the truth. In fact, it should more properly be called "butter-free" milk.

Years ago on the farm, buttermilk was the naturally soured liquid that remained after the butterfat was removed from whole milk or cream by churning. Today, buttermilk is made commercially by adding healthful bacteria to skim or 1% milk to produce the slightly sour buttermilk we use and enjoy in our cooking. One cup buttermilk has about the same number of calories as 1 cup skim or 1% milk (approximately 90 to 110 calories).

Today you can buy dry or powdered buttermilk, which needs only water added to it. Be sure to keep it in the refrigerator so it won't get lumpy, and it will last for several months.

You can also make your own buttermilk with a starter kit that can be purchased through kitchen specialty shops. The process is easy, and once you have created a batch with live bacteria, you can use a small amount from each batch to create new batches for as long as you like.

The process is similar to that used to make yogurt. In a heatproof container or saucepan, take 1 quart of either skim, 1%, 2% or whole milk, stir in 2 tablespoons dry skim milk and heat it to about 200° on a candy thermometer for at least 1 minute, to kill any bacteria. Place the container in a sink or another container of cold water. When the temperature reaches 75°, stir in the starter mixture (which contains "good" bacteria), pour mixture into a sterilized container and seal (canning jars work well for this). Keep the mixture around 75° for 1 day to allow the bacteria

to do its work, and you will end up with a delicious batch of buttermilk that you can use over and over again.

By varying the type of milk and time, you can control the flavor and consistency of the buttermilk to suit your personal tastes. If you have leftover buttermilk, it can be frozen. The next time you need it, just unthaw, stir until smooth and use.

An added benefit of making your own buttermilk is that the bacteria is alive and aids digestion, whereas the buttermilk you buy at the supermarket has been pasteurized after the milk has soured, and the healthful bacteria have been killed.

Whether you prefer to make your own or like the convenience of supermarket buttermilk, we think you will enjoy the delicious recipes we have compiled in this book.

LEMON PECAN BREAD

This loaf keeps well in the refrigerator for up to 1 month.

1 cup sugar
⅓ cup butter, softened
2 tsp. lemon extract
2 eggs
grated zest (peel, colored portion only) of 1 lemon
1½ cups flour
1 tsp. baking powder
1 tsp. salt
½ cup buttermilk
½ cup chopped pecans

GLAZE

⅓ cup fresh lemon juice
⅓ cup powdered sugar

Preheat oven to 350°. Grease a 9-x-5-inch loaf pan and line bottom with waxed paper. Using an electric mixer, beat sugar, butter and lemon extract until light. Add eggs, one at a time, and lemon zest. Sift together flour, baking powder and salt. Add to creamed mixture alternately with buttermilk. Fold in pecans. Pour into pan. Bake for 1 hour or until bread is firm in the center when pressed. Remove from oven and cool slightly.

Combine glaze ingredients and pour over bread while it is still warm.

Allow bread to cool completely in pan. Wrap tightly in foil and refrigerate overnight before serving.

Makes 1 loaf

AMAZING BUTTERMILK BREAD

This bread is amazing — it requires no kneading and no rising! The dough hook on an electric mixer works well for beating.

½ cup buttermilk
2½ tbs. butter
2 tbs. plus ¼ tsp. sugar
1 tsp. salt
1 pkg. fast-rising yeast
pinch ground ginger
¼ cup warm water
⅔ cup cold water
3 cups flour
¼ tsp. vinegar
½ tbs. butter, melted

Heat buttermilk, butter, 2 tbs. sugar and salt in a small saucepan until butter is melted; set aside. Combine yeast, ginger and ¼ tsp. sugar in warm water to dissolve yeast. Allow to stand until frothy, about 5 minutes . Place buttermilk mixture in a large bowl and add cold water. Stir in 1 cup flour. Add vinegar to yeast mixture and add to batter. Beat well. Add remaining flour and stir for 5 minutes. Oil a 9-x-5-inch loaf pan. Spread batter in pan using a wet spatula and smooth the top. Place pan in a cold oven and turn heat to 325°. Bake for 30 minutes. Brush with melted butter. Continue baking for another 45 minutes or until loaf sounds hollow when tapped on the bottom.

Makes 1 loaf

IRISH SODA BREAD

This classic Irish favorite, baked in the oven in a cast iron skillet, is traditionally slashed across the top with a cross before baking to scare away the devil.

¼ cup butter
3 cups flour
1½ tsp. salt
1 tbs. baking powder
1 tsp. baking soda
¾ cup sugar
1½ cups dried currants
1¾ cups buttermilk
2 eggs, beaten
2 tbs. butter, melted and cooled
1 tbs. caraway seeds, optional

Preheat oven to 350°. Grease a 10-inch cast iron skillet with 2 tbs. butter. In a large bowl, combine flour, salt, baking powder, soda and sugar. Add currants and stir to coat with flour. In a small bowl, combine buttermilk, eggs and 2 tbs. melted butter. Pour over dry ingredients and stir just to mix. Add caraway seeds. Spoon batter into skillet and dot the top with remaining butter. Bake for 1 hour or until puffed and golden. Cool in skillet for 10 minutes; remove to a wire rack. Cut in wedges to serve.

Makes 1 loaf

WHOLE WHEAT RAISIN BREAD

This is a hearty bread for sandwiches or for toasting.

1 pkg. active dry yeast
1/4 cup warm water
1/4 cup honey
1 1/2 cups buttermilk
3 tbs. butter
2 tsp. salt
3 1/2 cups whole wheat flour
1/2 tsp. baking soda
1/2 cup raisins

Dissolve yeast in warm water. Add honey and allow to stand until foamy. Heat buttermilk and butter until butter just melts. Stir into yeast mixture. In a separate bowl, combine salt, flour and soda. Add raisins. Pour in yeast mixture and beat until smooth.

Set bowl in a pan of warm water. Cover with a towel and allow to rise in a warm place until doubled in bulk, about 1 hour. Beat dough for 3 minutes. Grease a 9-x-5-inch bread pan. Shape dough into a loaf and place in pan. Place pan in warm water and allow to rise until dough is 1 inch above top of pan. Put pan in a cold oven. Turn heat to 400° and bake for 15 minutes. Reduce heat to 325° and continue baking for 30 to 35 minutes or until loaf sounds hollow when tapped on the bottom. Turn out on a wire rack to cool.

Makes 1 loaf

PRUNE BREAD

Try serving this with whipped cream cheese.

2 cups sugar
1 cup vegetable oil
3 eggs, beaten
1 cup buttermilk
1 lb. prunes, pitted and
  chopped

2½ cups flour
2 tsp. baking soda
½ tsp. ground cloves
1 tsp. cinnamon
1 tsp. salt

Preheat oven to 325°. Grease two 9-x-5-inch bread pans. In a large bowl, stir together sugar, oil and eggs. Add buttermilk and combine. Stir in prunes. Sift together dry ingredients and add to wet ingredients. Divide batter evenly into pans. Bake for 1 hour. Cool loaves on a wire rack.

Makes 2 loaves

BLUEBERRY CORNBREAD

Serve piping hot with honey butter.

1 1/4 cups flour
3/4 cup yellow cornmeal
1/3 cup sugar
2 tsp. baking powder
1/2 tsp. salt

1 cup buttermilk
1 egg, beaten
5 tbs. butter, melted
1 1/2 cups fresh blueberries

Preheat oven to 400°. Grease an 8-inch baking pan. In a large bowl, combine flour, cornmeal, sugar, baking powder and salt. In a small bowl, combine buttermilk, egg and butter; stir into dry ingredients. Do not overmix. Gently fold in blueberries. Spread batter into pan and bake for 20 to 25 minutes or until a toothpick inserted in the center comes out clean.

Makes 8 servings

UPSIDE-DOWN BREAKFAST CORNBREAD

This special cornbread is a feast for the eyes as well as the palate, with spicy sausage links and apples baked right on top.

8 oz. pork sausage links
4 tbs. butter
½ cup brown sugar, firmly packed
3 medium apples, peeled and cored,
each cut into 8 wedges
1 cup flour
¾ cup yellow cornmeal
¼ cup brown sugar, firmly packed
1 tbs. baking powder
1 tsp. salt
1 egg, beaten
¼ cup butter, melted
1 cup buttermilk
maple syrup

Preheat oven to 400°. Grease a 9-inch baking pan. In a skillet, brown sausages until cooked. Remove and set aside. Pour off all but 2 tbs. drippings. Add butter and brown sugar to skillet and stir until melted. Add apple wedges and cook until tender, about 10 minutes. Place sausages and apples on bottom of baking pan, arranging them attractively. Pour any juices from skillet over apples and sausages.

To prepare cornbread: Combine flour, cornmeal, brown sugar, baking powder and salt. In a small bowl, combine egg, butter and buttermilk. Pour over flour mixture and mix well. Spread batter over apples and sausages and bake for 20 to 25 minutes.

Invert onto a serving platter. Cut into squares and serve with maple syrup.

Makes 8 servings

SPOONBREAD CASSEROLE

Spoonbread is so soft it must be eaten with a spoon.

2 cups yellow cornmeal
1⅓ cups flour
⅓ cup sugar
1 tsp. salt
2 tsp. baking soda
2 tsp. baking powder

2½ cups milk
2½ cups buttermilk
4 eggs, beaten
1 can (17 oz.) creamed corn
¼ tsp. Tabasco Sauce
4 tbs. butter

Preheat oven to 400°. In a large bowl, combine cornmeal, flour, sugar, salt, soda and baking powder. Add 1½ cups milk, 1½ cups buttermilk and eggs. Whisk in corn and Tabasco. Place butter in a 9-x-13-inch pan and place in oven. When butter melts, pour batter into pan. Carefully pour remaining milk and buttermilk over top; do not stir. Bake for 30 to 40 minutes or until puffed and golden. Allow to stand for 15 minutes.

Makes 12 servings

CORN STICKS

These are fun to make using a special cast iron corn stick pan, shaped like ears of corn.

1½ cups yellow cornmeal
¼ cup flour
1 tbs. sugar
1 tsp. baking powder
½ tsp. baking soda

½ tsp. salt
1 cup buttermilk
1 egg, beaten
2 tbs. vegetable oil

Preheat oven to 400°. Grease a cast iron corn stick pan well. Heat in oven for 5 minutes. In a bowl, combine cornmeal, flour, sugar, baking powder, soda and salt. In another bowl, combine buttermilk, egg and oil; add to dry ingredients and stir until just moistened. Spoon batter into hot pan, filling ⅔ full. Bake for 12 to 15 minutes or until corn sticks are lightly browned.

Makes 14

BUTTERMILK CINNAMON ROLLS

The orange cream cheese glaze makes a perfect topping for these wonderful cinnamon rolls.

DOUGH

2 pkg. active dry yeast
¼ cup warm water
1 tbs. sugar
1½ cups buttermilk
2 tbs. sugar

1 tsp. salt
½ tsp. baking soda
½ cup vegetable oil
4½ cups flour

FILLING

½ cup butter, melted
1½ cups brown sugar, firmly
   packed

2 tsp. cinnamon
grated zest (peel, colored
   portion only) of 2 oranges

GLAZE

4 oz. cream cheese
1 cup powdered sugar

juice of 2 oranges

Dissolve yeast in warm water with 1 tbs. sugar. Allow to stand for 5 minutes. Heat buttermilk until warm. Stir in 2 tbs. sugar, salt, soda, oil, flour and yeast mixture. Knead 15 times on a lightly floured surface. Cover and allow to rise for 15 minutes. Roll dough into a 10-x-18-inch rectangle.

Combine filling ingredients in a small bowl.

Sprinkle dough with filling. Roll up dough rectangle, starting from long end. Cut into 1½-inch pieces and place cut side up in a buttered 9-x-13-inch baking pan. Allow to rise for 30 minutes. Bake rolls at 400° for 10 to 15 minutes.

While rolls are cooling slightly, combine glaze ingredients in a small bowl. Pour over warm rolls.

Makes 12 servings

BUTTERMILK COFFEE CAKE

This very tender coffee cake is quick and easy to prepare for a breakfast crowd.

1½ cups sugar
¾ cup butter, softened
3 eggs
1½ cups buttermilk
2 tsp. vanilla extract
3⅓ cups flour
1½ tbs. baking powder

TOPPING

1 cup butter, chilled and cut into slices
1½ cups brown sugar, firmly packed
1½ cups chopped walnuts or pecans
1 tsp. cinnamon

Preheat oven to 375°. Grease a 9-x-13-inch baking pan. By hand or with an electric mixer, food processor or blender, combine sugar, butter, eggs, buttermilk and vanilla until smooth and light. Add flour and baking powder, mixing well. Pour into pan.

Combine topping ingredients until crumbly. Sprinkle over top of batter.

Bake for 35 minutes or until a toothpick inserted in the center comes out clean.

Makes 12 servings

BUTTERMILK BISCUITS

Purists say you should sift the dry ingredients 4 times!

2 cups flour
2 tsp. baking powder
1 tsp. salt
½ tsp. baking soda

¼ tsp. cream of tartar
¼ cup vegetable shortening
1 cup buttermilk

Sift together flour, baking powder, salt, soda and cream of tartar. Cut in shortening using 2 knives or a pastry blender, until mixture resembles cornmeal. Stir in buttermilk and mix until smooth. Roll out with a lightly floured rolling pin on a lightly floured board until dough is ½-inch thick. Cut biscuits using a floured biscuit cutter, pressing straight down without twisting. Grease a baking sheet and place biscuits upside down, 1 inch apart. Bake at 450° for 12 to 15 minutes or until light golden brown.

Makes 10-12

FRUITED BRUNCH MOLD

This is something different and refreshing for brunch.

1 pkg. unflavored gelatin
1 cup buttermilk
1 cup orange juice
3 tbs. honey
1½ cups cubed cantaloupe

2 fresh peaches, peeled,
  pitted and sliced
1 cup sliced strawberries
½ cup chopped walnuts
fresh fruit for garnish

In a food processor or blender, sprinkle gelatin over buttermilk and allow to stand for 5 minutes to soften. Heat orange juice to boiling and add to gelatin mixture with honey; blend. Pour into a bowl, cover and chill until syrupy. Fold in fruits and nuts and pour into a 1-quart mold. Refrigerate overnight. To unmold, dip in warm water for 30 seconds and run a knife around edge of mold. Invert onto a serving plate. Garnish with fresh fruit.

Makes 6 servings

RASPBERRY BUTTERMILK MUFFINS

Use only fresh raspberries for a real taste bud treat.

2 cups flour
½ cup sugar
2 tsp. baking powder
1 tsp. salt
6 tbs. butter
1 egg, beaten

1 cup buttermilk
1 cup fresh raspberries
½ cup chopped pecans
1 tbs. sugar
1 tsp. cinnamon

Preheat oven to 400°. Line 12 muffin cups with paper liners. In a bowl, combine flour, sugar, baking powder and salt. In a small bowl, combine butter, egg and buttermilk. Stir into dry ingredients until just moistened. Gently fold in raspberries and pecans. Spoon batter into cups. Combine sugar and cinnamon and sprinkle on muffin tops. Bake for 20 to 25 minutes or until golden. Serve hot.

Makes 12 servings

RAISIN ORANGE MUFFINS

These incredibly moist muffins burst with orange flavor.

½ cup butter
1 cup sugar
2 eggs
1 tsp. baking soda
1 cup buttermilk
2 cups flour

grated zest (peel, colored portion only) of 2 oranges
½ cup golden raisins
juice of 2 oranges
1 cup brown sugar, firmly packed

Preheat oven to 400°. Line 12 muffin cups with paper liners. In a large bowl, cream butter and sugar. Add eggs; beat until well mixed. Dissolve soda in buttermilk; add to butter mixture alternately with flour. Stir in orange zest and raisins. Spoon batter into cups. Bake for 20 to 25 minutes or until golden. In a small bowl, combine orange juice with brown sugar. Remove muffins from oven; spoon orange juice mixture over each muffin.

Makes 12 servings

PARMESAN HERB MUFFINS

These are wonderful with soups, stews or chowders. Serve warm with butter.

2 cups flour
1 tsp. sugar
2 tsp. baking powder
½ tsp. dried oregano
½ tsp. dried basil
¼ tsp. garlic powder
½ tsp. baking soda
½ tsp. salt
1 cup freshly grated Parmesan cheese
½ cup chopped fresh parsley
1½ cups buttermilk
¼ cup olive oil
1 egg, beaten

Preheat oven to 400°. Line 12 muffin cups with paper liners. In a medium bowl, combine flour, sugar, baking powder, oregano, basil, garlic powder, soda, salt, Parmesan cheese and parsley. In a large bowl, combine buttermilk, olive oil and egg, mixing well; add to dry ingredients and stir until just moistened. Spoon into muffin cups. Bake for 20 minutes or until golden. Allow to cool in pan for 10 minutes.

Makes 12

6-WEEK BRAN MUFFINS

This batter will keep in the refrigerator for up to 6 weeks.

2 cups boiling water
5 tsp. baking soda
1 cup butter
2 cups sugar
4 eggs
4 cups All Bran cereal
2 cups Bran Flakes cereal

2 cups raisins
1 cup chopped walnuts,
  optional
1 qt. buttermilk
5 cups flour
1 tbs. salt

Mix boiling water with soda; cool. Cream butter, sugar and eggs until light. Combine with water mixture. Add cereals, raisins and nuts. Beat in buttermilk alternately with flour and salt. Pour batter into an airtight container and store in the refrigerator. When ready to bake, heat oven to 400°. Pour batter into greased muffin cups and bake for 20 minutes.

Makes 48

CORN MUFFINS WITH SUN-DRIED TOMATOES

If your grocer doesn't carry oil-packed sun-dried tomatoes, buy the dry-packed variety and soak them in oil before using.

1 cup yellow cornmeal
1 cup flour
1/3 cup sugar
2 1/2 tsp. baking powder
1/2 tsp. salt

1 cup buttermilk
1 large egg
6 tbs. butter, melted
1/2 cup chopped drained oil-
   packed sun-dried tomatoes

Preheat oven to 425°. Sift cornmeal, flour, sugar, baking powder and salt into a large bowl. Make a well in the center. In a small bowl, mix buttermilk, egg and butter; pour into well in dry ingredients. Stir until just combined; do not overmix. Gently fold in tomatoes. Line 10 muffin cups with paper liners. Divide batter evenly among cups. Bake for 20 minutes or until golden.

Makes 10

BUTTERMILK WAFFLES

Most waffles take about 3 to 4 minutes to cook. When ready, steam will stop coming out of the crack between the grids.

2 cups flour
2 tbs. brown sugar, firmly
   packed
1 tsp. baking soda
½ tsp. salt

2 cups buttermilk
2 eggs, separated
⅓ cup butter, melted and
   cooled

Preheat and grease the waffle iron. In a large bowl, combine flour, brown sugar, soda and salt. In another bowl, combine buttermilk, egg yolks and butter. Beat egg whites by hand or with a mixer until stiff. Add buttermilk mixture to flour mixture and blend well. Fold egg whites gently into batter.

Pour ⅓ cup batter for each waffle into waffle iron and bake until crisp and golden, about 2 minutes.

Makes twelve 5-inch waffles

OATMEAL BUTTERMILK PANCAKES

Prepare this batter ahead of time to take with you on camping trips. Be sure to keep batter cold and tightly covered.

2 cups oatmeal
2 cups buttermilk
3 eggs, beaten
2 tbs. sugar
¼ cup vegetable oil

½ cup flour
1 tsp. baking powder
1 tsp. baking soda
1 tsp. salt

In a large bowl, combine oatmeal and buttermilk. Cover and allow to stand at room temperature overnight. Add remaining ingredients and stir just to combine. Cook on a lightly greased hot griddle until bubbly and underside is golden brown. Turn once.

Makes 12

COTTAGE CHEESE PANCAKES
WITH BLUEBERRY SAUCE

These have a light and lovely flavor with a touch of lemon.

1 cup flour	1 egg
1 tsp. baking powder	2 tsp. sugar
1 tsp. baking soda	1 tsp. grated lemon zest
1 cup cottage cheese	(peel, colored portion only)
1 cup buttermilk	*Blueberry Sauce*, follows

Sift flour, baking powder and soda onto waxed paper. In a food processor or blender, combine cottage cheese, buttermilk, egg, sugar and lemon zest. Add flour mixture and process briefly to combine. Heat a large griddle and grease lightly. Pour batter onto griddle, using about ¼ cup for each pancake. Cook until bubbles form on the surface, about 2 to 3 minutes. Turn to cook other side, about 1 to 2 minutes. Remove and keep warm while

making additional pancakes. Serve with *Blueberry Sauce*.

Makes 12

BLUEBERRY SAUCE

1 tbs. cornstarch
3 tbs. sugar
2 cups fresh blueberries
2 tbs. fresh lemon juice
½ tsp. grated lemon zest (peel, colored portion only)

In a saucepan, combine cornstarch and sugar. Add remaining ingredients and bring to a boil over medium heat, stirring constantly. Lower heat and simmer for 5 minutes. Serve warm.

Makes 1½ cups

CORNMEAL AND BUTTERMILK HOTCAKES

A hint of sherry adds a nutty flavor to these flapjacks.

1 egg, separated
¾ cup buttermilk
1 tbs. butter, melted
2 tbs. cream sherry
⅔ cup flour

2 tbs. cornmeal
½ tsp. baking soda
½ tsp. baking powder
¼ tsp. salt

In a medium bowl, beat egg white until stiff peaks form. In a large bowl, combine egg yolk, buttermilk, butter and sherry. Add flour, cornmeal, soda, baking powder and salt; mix well. Gently fold in egg white. Preheat and butter a large griddle. Spoon batter, using ¼ cup for each hotcake, onto hot griddle. Spread batter to make a 3-inch circle. Cook until bubbles form on the surface; turn to cook other side.

Makes 12

CRÈME FRAÎCHE

This is wonderful in many sauces and soups and is so easy to make. It is also scrumptious over fresh fruit or warm pies.

1 cup whipping cream
2 tbs. buttermilk

Heat cream in a heavy saucepan to lukewarm, about 85° on a candy thermometer. Remove from heat and whisk in buttermilk. Cover and allow to stand in a warm place until slightly thickened, about 24 hours. Stir well, cover and refrigerate until ready to use.

Makes 1 cup

BUTTERMILK AND AVOCADO SALAD DRESSING

Try this dressing on your next taco salad.

2 very ripe black-skinned
avocados, peeled, seeded
and diced
½ cup mayonnaise
3 tbs. lemon juice

1½ cups buttermilk
2 green onions
1 tsp. salt
½ tsp. freshly ground
pepper

Combine all ingredients in a blender or food processor and blend until smooth. Pour into a container and place plastic wrap directly on dressing surface to prevent darkening. Refrigerate for at least 1 hour before serving.

Makes 3 cups

GORGONZOLA DRESSING

*This dressing makes an elegant salad with romaine lettuce
and garlic croutons.*

8 oz. cream cheese
½ cup mayonnaise
¼ tsp. salt
2 tsp. sugar
1 clove garlic, minced
½ cup buttermilk
6 oz. Gorgonzola cheese, cut into 1-inch cubes

In a blender or food processor, combine cream cheese, mayonnaise, salt, sugar, garlic and buttermilk and blend until smooth. Add Gorgonzola and process briefly, leaving cheese chunky. Cover and chill.

Makes 2 cups

CAULIFLOWER SALAD

Take this salad to your next potluck dinner party. Start preparing it the day before.

1 head cauliflower, cut into small pieces
6 green onions, thinly sliced
1 lb. bacon, fried crisp and crumbled
Quick Blue Cheese Dressing, follows
1 head iceberg lettuce, shredded

The day before serving, place cauliflower, green onions and bacon in a large, deep bowl. Frost with 1 cup dressing. Top with lettuce and remaining dressing. Cover with plastic wrap and refrigerate. Just before serving, toss thoroughly, adding more dressing if necessary.

Makes 6-8 servings

QUICK BLUE CHEESE DRESSING

4 oz. blue cheese, crumbled
1 cup buttermilk
1 cup mayonnaise
1 clove garlic, minced

Combine all ingredients and chill until ready to use.

Makes 2 cups

BUTTERMILK TARRAGON DRESSING

*Serve with a leaf lettuce salad with thinly sliced red onion,
sprinkled with toasted walnuts.*

½ cup buttermilk
¼ cup mayonnaise
1 clove garlic, minced
¼ tsp. salt
½ tsp. dry mustard
1 tsp. dried tarragon, crumbled
pepper

Combine all ingredients. Chill for several hours.

Makes ¾ cup

CHILLED RED PEPPER BISQUE

This rich soup has a beautiful color and splendid flavor.

2 tbs. butter
2 red bell peppers, chopped
2 cups chopped onion
1 cup chicken broth
2 cups buttermilk
salt and pepper
½ tsp. Tabasco Sauce

In a deep skillet, melt butter over medium heat. Sauté peppers and onion until very tender. Add chicken broth and simmer for 30 minutes. In a food processor or blender, puree vegetables and liquid. Add buttermilk, salt and pepper. Stir in Tabasco. Cover and chill for 4 hours or overnight. Serve cold.

Makes 6 servings

ICED CUCUMBER SOUP

This soup is just the thing for a hot summer day.

4 cups chicken broth
5 medium cucumbers,
  peeled, halved, seeded
  and chopped
1 cup buttermilk

2 tbs. thinly sliced green
  onion
salt
1 tsp. hot red pepper flakes
  for garnish

In a large soup pot, bring chicken broth to a boil. Add ¾ of the chopped cucumbers and simmer for 5 minutes. Cool slightly. In a food processor or blender, puree until smooth. Cover and chill. When cool, stir in buttermilk. To serve, add remaining cucumber, green onion and salt to taste. Serve in individual soup bowls. Garnish with hot red pepper flakes.

Makes 6-8 servings

CHILLED BUTTERMILK AND SHRIMP SOUP

Try this quick and delicious soup for lunch on the patio.
Serve icy cold in small bowls.

2 cucumbers, peeled, quartered lengthwise,
seeded and thinly sliced
$\frac{1}{2}$ cup thinly sliced green onions
3 tbs. chopped fresh dill
1 lb. baby shrimp
1 qt. buttermilk
salt and pepper

Combine all ingredients and season to taste. Cover and chill
overnight.

Makes 8 servings

CHEESE STUFFED CHICKEN BREASTS

Panko breadcrumbs are made out of rice flour and give a light and crispy coating. Look for them in the Oriental section of your grocery store. Any breadcrumbs can be substituted.

4 whole chicken breasts, skinned and boned
8 oz. cream cheese, room temperature
1 clove garlic, minced
1 tbs. dried dill
2 tbs. chopped fresh parsley
1 tsp. salt
½ tsp. white pepper
2 cups buttermilk
½ cup flour
2 cups panko breadcrumbs
¼ cup butter
2 tbs. vegetable oil

Lay chicken breasts flat and pound to an even thickness, about ½ inch. Set aside. In a small bowl, combine cream cheese, garlic, dill, parsley, salt and pepper. Divide mixture into fourths. Place each fourth on half of each chicken breast, fold other half over and press edges to seal cream cheese inside. Whisk together buttermilk and flour. Dip each breast into buttermilk mixture, and then into panko breadcrumbs. (At this point, chicken may be placed on a cookie sheet, covered with plastic wrap and refrigerated for up to 24 hours.) Melt butter in a large skillet over medium high heat, add oil and chicken breasts and brown on each side, about 5 minutes. Remove to a shallow ovenproof casserole. Bake at 350° for 30 minutes.

Makes 4 servings

BUTTERMILK MARINADE FOR GRILLED LAMB

We always get rave reviews when we serve this to company.

one 4-5 lb. leg of lamb, butterflied
1 cup buttermilk
2 tbs. lemon juice
½ cup red wine vinegar
½ cup Dijon mustard
½ cup finely chopped onion
2 cloves garlic, minced
1½ tsp. salt
1 tsp. dried oregano
1 tsp. dried basil
1 tsp. dried thyme
1 tsp. dried rosemary
½ tsp. pepper

Using a small, sharp knife, remove any excess fat, muscle or gristle from leg of lamb. Combine buttermilk with remaining ingredients to make marinade. Place lamb in a glass bowl. Pour marinade over lamb, turning to coat well. Refrigerate overnight, turning occasionally. Remove meat from marinade and allow to stand at room temperature for 1 hour before cooking. Grill or broil 6 inches from heat. Cook lamb for about 40 minutes for medium rare, turning occasionally. Slice on the diagonal to serve.

Makes 6-8 servings

NOTE: Lamb should really be served medium rare, but if you like it otherwise, use a meat thermometer: 160° for rare, 165° for medium rare, 170° for medium, 175° for well done.

HAZELNUT CHICKEN WITH BUTTERMILK GRAVY

To toast hazelnuts, spread them on a cookie sheet and toast at 350° for 10 to 15 minutes. Place in a clean dish towel and rub briskly to remove skins. Depending on the size of the chicken breasts, you may have nuts left over after breading that you can add to the gravy.

1 cup finely ground toasted hazelnuts
1 tsp. salt
½ tsp. pepper
3 whole chicken breasts, skinned, boned and halved
2 cups buttermilk
4 tbs. butter
4 tbs. vegetable oil

In a shallow dish, combine hazelnuts, salt and pepper. Dip chicken breasts first into 1 cup buttermilk, and then into nut mixture. Melt butter in a large skillet; add oil. Sauté chicken breasts over medium heat, turning once, until cooked through, about 10 minutes. Remove chicken breasts to a platter and keep warm. Add 1 cup buttermilk and any remaining nuts to skillet, bring to a boil and stir until mixture thickens. Serve with chicken.

Makes 6 servings

OLD-FASHIONED BUTTERMILK POT ROAST

Buttermilk adds tang to this recipe. Serve with mashed potatoes.

1 tbs. flour
1 tbs. dry mustard
1 tsp. salt
½ tsp. pepper
one 4 lb. beef pot roast, blade or rump
1 tbs. butter
1 tbs. vegetable oil
1 beef bouillon cube
1½ cups hot water
1½ cups buttermilk
6 medium carrots, peeled and cut into 1-inch chunks
1 pkg. (10 oz.) frozen Brussels sprouts
⅓ cup flour

Combine flour, mustard, salt and pepper and rub into roast. Heat a large Dutch oven and brown meat in butter and oil. Dissolve bouillon cube in hot water and pour over roast. Cover with a tight-fitting lid and simmer for 1½ hours. Add ½ cup buttermilk, carrots and Brussels sprouts to pan. Cover and continue to simmer for another hour. Before serving, remove roast and vegetables to a platter and keep warm. Reserve drippings. In a small bowl, whisk together remaining buttermilk and flour until smooth. Add to pan drippings and stir constantly over medium heat until gravy is thickened and bubbly. Serve gravy with roast and vegetables.

Makes 6 servings

SPICY FRIED CHICKEN

Fried chicken loses its texture when refrigerated.

1½ cups flour
2 tsp. cayenne pepper
1 tsp. chili powder
1 tsp. onion powder
1 tsp. salt
½ tsp. poultry seasoning

1 cup buttermilk
1 egg, beaten
vegetable oil for frying
1 frying chicken, about
   3½ lb., cut into pieces

In a locking food storage bag, combine flour and seasonings. In a shallow dish, combine buttermilk and egg . Pour 1 inch oil into an electric skillet and heat to 325°. Shake 2 to 3 pieces chicken at a time in bag. Dip into buttermilk mixture and shake bag again. Repeat with remaining pieces. Fry chicken in hot oil for 20 to 25 minutes or until cooked through and browned. Drain on paper towels.

Makes 4 servings

BUTTERMILK PIE CRUST

This recipe produces a tender, flaky crust every time and the dough can be frozen for up to 1 month.

2½ cups flour
2 tbs. sugar
1 tsp. salt
½ cup butter, chilled and cut into slices

½ cup vegetable shortening, chilled
¼ cup plus 2 tbs. buttermilk

In a large bowl, food processor or blender, combine flour, sugar and salt. Cut in butter and shortening using a pastry blender, or process briefly. Mixture should resemble cottage cheese. Add buttermilk and combine until mixture forms moist clumps. Gather into a ball and divide in half. Flatten into disks, wrap in plastic and chill for 1 hour. Allow dough to stand at room temperature to soften slightly before using.

Makes 2 crusts

OLD-FASHIONED GINGERBREAD

Serve with big glasses of cold milk.

2¾ cups flour
1 tsp. baking soda
¾ tsp. salt
1 tbs. ground ginger
¾ tsp. ground nutmeg
½ tsp. cinnamon
¼ tsp. ground cloves
1 cup light molasses
½ cup butter
½ cup brown sugar, firmly packed
¾ cup buttermilk
2 eggs, beaten
2 tbs. orange juice
2 tbs. brandy

In a large bowl, combine flour, soda, salt and spices. Place molasses, butter and brown sugar in a saucepan over medium heat and bring to a boil. Cook, stirring constantly, until sugar dissolves. Allow to cool slightly and add to flour mixture. Add buttermilk, eggs, orange juice and brandy. Stir until smooth. Pour batter into a greased, floured 9-x-13-inch baking pan. Bake at 350° for 25 to 30 minutes or until a toothpick inserted in the center comes out clean. Allow to cool completely in pan on a wire rack.

Makes 12 servings

BUTTERMILK PIE

*A favorite from down South. This tastes great in **Buttermilk Pie Crust**, page 53.*

¼ cup butter, softened	½ cup buttermilk
1 cup sugar	⅛ tsp. ground nutmeg
1 tsp. flour	½ tsp. vanilla extract
3 eggs, beaten	one 8-inch pie shell, unbaked

Cream together butter, sugar and flour. Slowly add eggs, mixing well. Add buttermilk, nutmeg and vanilla and pour into pie shell. Bake at 400° for 30 to 40 minutes or until pie is set — no liquid will be in the center — and golden.

Makes 6-8 servings

BUTTERMILK PIE WITH PECANS AND COCONUT

The coconut and pecans make this delectable pie both chewy and crunchy.

1 cup sugar
2 tbs. flour
¼ tsp. grated nutmeg
3 eggs
1 cup buttermilk
⅓ cup butter, melted

1 tsp. vanilla extract
one 9-inch pie shell,
 prebaked
½ cup flaked coconut
½ cup chopped pecans

Preheat oven to 350°. By hand or with an electric mixer, combine sugar, flour, nutmeg and eggs. Blend in buttermilk, butter and vanilla until smooth. Pour into pie crust; sprinkle with coconut and nuts. Bake for 45 minutes or until filling is set — no liquid will be in the center. Cool and serve at room temperature.

Makes 8 servings

CHOCOLATE BUTTERMILK CAKE

One baker's secret — a cake will begin to smell just before it is done. It will also pull away from the sides of the pan and be springy in the center when pressed.

2 cups flour
2 cups sugar
1 tsp. baking soda
1 tsp. cinnamon
4 tbs. unsweetened cocoa
1 cup butter
1 cup water
2 eggs
½ cup buttermilk
1 tsp. vanilla extract
Frosting, follows

Preheat oven to 400°. In a large bowl, combine flour, sugar, soda and cinnamon. In a medium saucepan, combine cocoa, butter and water. Cook over medium heat until butter is melted. Stir into dry ingredients. Add eggs, buttermilk and vanilla and mix well. Grease an 11-x-14-inch baking pan. Pour batter into pan. Bake for 15 to 20 minutes or until cake tests done when a toothpick inserted in the center comes out clean. Pour *Frosting* immediately over cake as it comes from the oven.

Makes 12-16 servings

FROSTING

½ cup butter
6 tbs. buttermilk
4 tbs. unsweetened cocoa

1 lb. powdered sugar
1 cup chopped walnuts
1 tsp. vanilla extract

In a medium saucepan, combine butter and buttermilk. Stir over medium heat until butter is melted. Add remaining ingredient and stir well to combine.

BUTTERMILK FUDGE

This delicious candy tastes much like old-fashioned penuche.
It keeps well in the freezer for up to 6 months.

1 cup buttermilk
1 tsp. baking soda
2 cups sugar
¾ cup butter
2 tbs. light corn syrup
2 cups broken pecans
1½ tsp. vanilla extract

Combine buttermilk and soda in a heavy 4-quart saucepan. Stir to dissolve soda. Add sugar, butter and corn syrup. Turn heat to medium high, stirring constantly until mixture starts to boil. Use a wet paper towel to remove any grains of sugar on sides of saucepan. Lower heat, insert a candy thermometer and boil

gently until temperature reaches 244°. Remove saucepan from heat and stir in pecans and vanilla. Mixture will thicken quickly. Drop by teaspoonfuls onto an oiled cookie sheet. Candy will harden as it cools.

Makes about 40 pieces

GARDEN PATCH COOKIES

These yummy cookies are also very nutritious.

²/₃ cup butter
1¼ cups brown sugar, firmly packed
2 eggs
1 tsp. vanilla extract
1 tbs. grated lemon zest (peel, colored portion only)
½ cup buttermilk
2 cups flour
1 tsp. baking powder
1 tsp. baking soda
1 tsp. salt
1 tsp. cinnamon
½ tsp. ground nutmeg

2 cups oatmeal
1 cup raisins
1 cup chopped walnuts
1 cup shredded carrots
1 cup shredded zucchini

Preheat oven to 400°. Cream together butter, brown sugar, eggs, vanilla, lemon zest and buttermilk. Sift together flour, baking powder, soda, salt, cinnamon and nutmeg. Add to creamed mixture. Stir in oatmeal, raisins, nuts, carrots and zucchini. Drop dough by spoonfuls onto greased cookie sheets. Bake for about 12 minutes or until golden.

Makes 5 dozen

KENTUCKY BUTTER CAKE

*A hot butter sauce poured over the cake makes it exception-
ally moist and rich. Try using dark rum in the **Butter Sauce**
instead of water.*

1 cup butter, room temperature
2 cups sugar
4 eggs
1 cup buttermilk
2 tsp. vanilla extract
3 cups flour
1 tsp. baking powder
$\frac{1}{2}$ tsp. baking soda
$\frac{1}{2}$ tsp. salt
Butter Sauce, follows

Preheat oven to 325°. By hand or with an electric mixer, cream butter and sugar until fluffy. Beat eggs into mixture one at a time, beating well after each addition. Stir in buttermilk and vanilla. Sift together flour, baking powder, soda and salt. Add to butter mixture; combine well. Pour into a greased tube or Bundt pan. Bake for 60 to 65 minutes or until cake tests done when a toothpick inserted in the center comes out clean. Make *Butter Sauce*. Pierce entire surface of cake with a fork and pour sauce over cake. Allow to cool.

Makes 12 servings

BUTTER SAUCE

1 cup sugar   ½ cup butter
¼ cup water   1 tbs. vanilla extract

Combine ingredients in a saucepan and cook, stirring constantly, until mixture is smooth and hot. Do not boil.

FAVORITE BANANA CAKE

When bananas get overly ripe, put them in the freezer, skins and all. To make this delicious cake, just thaw bananas in the microwave and peel.

½ cup butter
1½ cups sugar
2 eggs
1 cup mashed ripe bananas
1 tsp. vanilla extract
¼ cup buttermilk
1¾ cups flour
1 tsp. baking soda
1 tsp. baking powder
½ tsp. salt
1 cup chopped walnuts
Cream Cheese Icing, follows

Preheat oven to 350°. Grease a 9-x-13-inch baking pan. By hand or with a food processor, blender or electric mixer, cream butter and sugar until fluffy. Add eggs, bananas, vanilla and buttermilk. Sift together flour, soda, baking powder and salt; combine with banana mixture. Stir in walnuts. Spread batter into pan and bake for 30 minutes or until a toothpick inserted in the center comes out clean. Cool and frost with *Cream Cheese Icing*.

Makes 12-16 servings

CREAM CHEESE ICING

8 oz. cream cheese	2 cups powdered sugar
½ cup butter	1 tsp. vanilla extract

Using an electric mixer or food processor, beat ingredients until creamy.

ORANGE CAKE

This dark and delicious cake is loaded with flavor.

1 large orange, peeled
1 cup walnuts
1 cup dark raisins
1 cup sugar
½ cup butter
2 eggs
1 tsp. vanilla extract

2 cups flour
1 tsp. baking soda
1 tsp. baking powder
½ tsp. salt
1 cup buttermilk
Frosting, follows

Using a food processor or blender, chop orange, walnuts and raisins until finely minced. Remove mixture and reserve 2 tbs. for *Frosting*. Preheat oven to 350°. Grease a 9-x-13-inch baking pan. By hand or with an electric mixer, beat sugar, butter, eggs and vanilla until light. Sift together flour, soda, baking powder and salt. Add to creamed mixture alternately with buttermilk, mixing well. Add orange mixture to batter. Pour into pan and bake for 40 to 45 minutes or until a toothpick inserted in the center comes out clean. Cool in pan. Spread *Frosting* on cooled cake.

Makes 12 servings

FROSTING

8 oz. cream cheese, room
 temperature
1 cup powdered sugar
1 tsp. vanilla extract

2 tbs. milk
2 tbs. reserved orange
 mixture

Combine cream cheese, sugar, vanilla and milk; beat until light. Stir in reserved orange mixture.

CLASSIC GERMAN SWEET CHOCOLATE CAKE

This has been a permanent favorite in our family for years.

1 pkg. (4 oz.) German sweet
  chocolate
½ cup boiling water
1 cup butter
2 cups sugar
4 egg yolks
1 tsp. vanilla extract
2½ cups cake flour

1 tsp. baking soda
½ tsp. salt
1 cup buttermilk
4 egg whites, stiffly beaten
Coconut Pecan Frosting,
  follows
whipped cream, optional

Preheat oven to 350°. Line three 9-inch layer pans with parchment paper. Melt chocolate in boiling water; cool. By hand or with an electric mixer, cream butter and sugar until light. Add egg yolks, one at a time, beating well after each addition. Add vanilla and chocolate. Sift flour with soda and salt. Add alternately ⅓ at a time with buttermilk, beating until smooth. Gently fold in

egg whites. Divide batter evenly into pans. Bake for 30 to 35 minutes or until a toothpick inserted in the center comes out clean. Cool. Frost only tops of layers with *Coconut Pecan Frosting*. If desired, frost sides with whipped cream and store in the refrigerator.

Makes 12 servings

COCONUT PECAN FROSTING

1 cup evaporated milk	1 tsp. vanilla extract
1 cup sugar	1⅓ cups coconut
3 egg yolks, beaten	1 cup chopped pecans
½ cup butter	

Combine evaporated milk, sugar, egg yolks, butter and vanilla in a heavy saucepan. Cook over medium heat until thickened, stirring, for about 12 minutes. Add coconut and pecans. Cool until spreading consistency, stirring occasionally.

CARROT CAKE

This cake keeps well and is packed with good things. It can also be frozen.

5 eggs
3 cups sugar
1 cup vegetable oil
1 cup buttermilk
1 tbs. vanilla extract
3 cups flour
1 tbs. baking soda
1 tbs. cinnamon
½ tsp. salt
3 cups shredded carrots, firmly packed
1 can (20 oz.) crushed pineapple, drained
1½ cups chopped walnuts
1½ cups shredded coconut
Buttermilk Topping, follows

Preheat oven to 325°. Grease a 9-x-13-inch baking pan. In a large bowl, combine eggs, sugar, oil, buttermilk and vanilla. Add flour, soda, cinnamon and salt. Stir in carrots, pineapple, nuts and coconut. Spread batter in pan and bake for 1 hour. Pour hot *Buttermilk Topping* over cake.

Makes 12 servings

BUTTERMILK TOPPING

1 cup sugar
½ cup butter
½ cup buttermilk
½ tsp. salt
1 tbs. corn syrup
1 tsp. vanilla extract

Combine ingredients in a saucepan and bring to a boil. Reduce heat and simmer for 10 minutes.

FOOD PROCESSOR FRUIT SHERBET

Use any type of summer berries you like including blue-berries, raspberries, strawberries or blackberries.

1 pt. frozen unsweetened berries
½ cup buttermilk
honey or low calorie sweetener, optional

Using a food processor or blender, combine berries with ¼ cup buttermilk. Process until berries are coarsely chopped. Add sweetener. Stir mixture with a spoon to redistribute. Cover and carefully add remaining buttermilk. Process until mixture has the texture of soft-serve ice cream. Serve immediately.

Makes 4 servings

BUTTERMILK ICE MILK

This is a light and refreshing dessert. Top it with fresh berries or your favorite sauce.

1 cup superfine sugar
¼ cup lemon juice
1 tsp. lemon zest (peel, colored portion only)
⅛ tsp. salt
2 cups buttermilk

Combine sugar, lemon juice, zest, salt and buttermilk, stirring until sugar is dissolved. Chill until cold and freeze in an ice cream maker according to the manufacturer's instructions.

Makes 8 servings

INDEX

Avocado and buttermilk salad dressing 36

Banana cake, favorite 66
Biscuits, buttermilk 22
Blue cheese dressing, quick 39
Blueberry
  cornbread 13
  sauce 33
Bran muffins, 6-week 28
Bread
  amazing buttermilk 6
  Irish soda 8
  lemon pecan 4
  prune 12
  whole wheat raisin 10
Butter sauce 65
Buttermilk
  about 1-3
  dry 2
  making 2-3
  powdered 2
Buttermilk topping 73

Cake
  buttermilk coffee 20
  carrot 72
  chocolate buttermilk 58
  classic German sweet chocolate 70
  favorite banana 66
  Kentucky butter 64
  orange 68
Carrot cake 72
Cauliflower salad 38
Chicken
  hazelnut, with buttermilk gravy 48
  spicy fried 52
Chocolate buttermilk cake 58
Cinnamon rolls, buttermilk 18
Coconut pecan frosting 71
Coffee cake, buttermilk 20
Cookies, garden patch 62
Corn muffins with sun-dried tomatoes 29
Corn sticks 17
Cornbread
  blueberry 13
  upside-down breakfast 14
Cornmeal and buttermilk hotcakes 34
Cottage cheese pancakes with blueberry sauce 32
Crème fraîche 35
Cucumber soup, iced 42

Dressing
  buttermilk and
    avocado salad 36
  buttermilk tarragon 40
  Gorgonzola 37
  quick blue cheese 39

Entrées
  buttermilk marinade
    for grilled lamb 46
  hazelnut chicken with
    buttermilk gravy 48
  old-fashioned butter-
    milk pot roast 50
  spicy fried chicken 52

Fried chicken, spicy 52
Fruit sherbet, food
  processor 74
Fruited brunch mold 23
Fudge, buttermilk 60

Garden patch cookies 62
German sweet chocolate
  cake, classic 70
Gingerbread, old-
  fashioned 54
Gorgonzola dressing 37

Hazelnut chicken with
  buttermilk gravy 48

Ice milk, buttermilk 75
Irish soda bread 8

Kentucky butter cake 64

Lamb, buttermilk mari-
  nade for grilled 46
Lemon pecan bread 4

Muffins
  6-week bran 28
  corn, with sun-dried
    tomatoes 29

Parmesan herb 26
raisin orange 25
raspberry buttermilk 24

Oatmeal buttermilk
  pancakes 31
Orange cake 68

Pancakes and hotcakes
  cornmeal and butter-
    milk 34
  cottage cheese pan-
    cakes with blueberry
    sauce 32
  oatmeal buttermilk 31
Parmesan herb muffins 26
Pecans and coconut,
  buttermilk pie with 57
Pie
  buttermilk 56
  buttermilk, with pecans
    and coconut 57
  crust, buttermilk 53

Pot roast, old-
  fashioned buttermilk 50
Prune bread 12

Raisin orange muffins 25
Raspberry buttermilk
  muffins 24
Red pepper bisque,
  chilled 41
Rolls, buttermilk
  cinnamon 18

Sherbet, food processor
  fruit 74
Shrimp and buttermilk
  soup, chilled 43
Soup(s)
  chilled buttermilk and
    shrimp soup 43
  chilled red pepper
    bisque 41
  iced cucumber 42
Spoonbread casserole 16

Tarragon dressing,
  buttermilk 40

Upside-down breakfast
  cornbread 14

Waffles, buttermilk 30
Whole wheat raisin
  bread 10